BABY ANIMALS

SUPER CUTE Kittens

AMY CULLIFORD

A Crabtree Roots Plus Book

Crabtree Publishing
crabtreebooks.com

School-to-Home Support for Caregivers and Teachers

This book helps children grow by letting them practice reading. Here are a few guiding questions to help the reader with building his or her comprehension skills. Possible answers appear here in red.

Before Reading:

- What do I think this book is about?
    - *I think this book is about cute kittens.*
    - *I think this book is about the kind of trouble kittens can get into.*
- What do I want to learn about this topic?
    - *I want to learn more about how to take care of kittens.*
    - *I want to learn what kinds of things kittens like to play with.*

During Reading:

- I wonder why...
    - *I wonder why kittens need lots of sleep.*
    - *I wonder why kittens drink milk from their mother.*
- What have I learned so far?
    - *I have learned that a kitten is a baby cat.*
    - *I have learned that kittens can jump and land on all four feet.*

After Reading:

- What details did I learn about this topic?
    - *I have learned that kittens use their claws to climb things.*
    - *I have learned that all kittens say meow!*
- Read the book again and look for the vocabulary words.
    - *I see the word **litter** on page 4 and the word **whiskers** on page 9. The other vocabulary words are found on page 23.*

A **kitten** is a baby cat.

When a mother cat has more than one kitten, it is called a **litter**.

There are many different kinds of kittens.

Some kittens are big, and some kittens are small.

Many kittens have long **tails**.

All kittens have **whiskers**.

When kittens are young, they drink their mother's milk.

When they start to grow, they eat cat food.

All kittens need lots of sleep!

Kittens also love to run and play.

They play with cat toys.

Kittens can jump and land on all four feet.

They can also climb things using their **claws**.

A **vet** helps to make sure a kitten is well.

All kittens say, *meow*!

Word List

Sight Words

a
all
also
and
are
baby
big
called
different
can
cat
climb
drink

eat
food
four
grow
has
have
helps
is
jump
kinds
long
lots
love

make
many
milk
more
mother
need
of
on
one
play
run
sleep
small

some
start
than
their
there
they
things
to
when
with
young

Words to Know

claws

kitten

litter

tails

vet

whiskers

BABY ANIMALS

SUPER CUTE Kittens

Written by: Amy Culliford

Designed by: Kathy Walsh

Series Development: James Earley

Proofreader: Melissa Boyce

Educational Consultant: Marie Lemke M.Ed.

Photographs:
Shutterstock: cover & title pg: ©Pewara Nicropithak, © Dmitry Kalinovsky; pg 3 & 23©Utekhina Anna; pg 5 & 23 ©Dora Zett; pg 6 ©Dora Zett, ©Eric Isselee; pg 7 ©PHOTOCREO Michal Bednarek, ©Cherry-Merry; pg 8 & 23 ©Ermolaev Alexander; pg 9 & 23 ©mama_mia; pg 10 ©Smile19; pg 11 ©Ermolaev Alexander; pg 12 © Pixel-Shot; pg 13 ©Rita_Kochmarjova; pg 14 ©Katrin Baidimirova; pg 15 ©Tony Campbell; pg 17 & 23 ©Andrii Yalanskyi; pg 19 & 23 ©Elnur; pg 21 ©Christian Mueller

Crabtree Publishing

crabtreebooks.com 800.387.7650

Printed in the U.S.A./012023/CG20220815

Published in Canada
Crabtree Publishing
616 Welland Ave
St. Catharines, Ontario
L2M 5V6

Published in the United States
Crabtree Publishing
347 Fifth Ave
Suite 1402-145
New York, NY 10016

Library and Archives Canada Cataloguing in Publication
Available at Library and Archives Canada

Library of Congress Cataloging-in-Publication Data
Available at the Library of Congress

Hardcover: 978-1-0396-9631-0
Paperback: 978-1-0396-9738-6
Ebook (pdf): 978-1-0396-9952-6
Epub: 978-1-0396-9845-1